Overview *Brave Little Snail*

Little Snail explores the garden.

Reading Vocabulary Words

slide
garden
brave

High-Frequency Words

the   he
likes   looks
to   down
not   oh

Building Future Vocabulary

*These vocabulary words do not appear in this text. They are provided
to develop related oral vocabulary that first appears in future texts.*

Words:	*back*	*move*	*compare*
Levels:	Yellow	Turquoise	Gold

Comprehension Strategy
Making and confirming
predictions

Fluency Skill
Adjusting pace

Phonics Skill
Initial sounds: short *u* (<u>u</u>p)

Reading-Writing Connection
Copying a phrase from
the book

...ᴏof the Flying
Colors Take-Home books for children to share with their families.

Differentiated Instruction
Before reading the text, query children to discover their level of understanding of the comprehension
strategy — Making and confirming
predictions. As you work together,
provide additional support to
children who show a beginning
mastery of the strategy.

Focus on ELL

• Ask children if they have ever
  had a garden. Have them share
  what their gardens were like
  and what they grew.

• Ask children to predict what
  Little Snail might encounter in
  the garden. Remind them that
  snails are very small and can
  only reach low things.

T1

Using This Teaching Version

1. Before Reading

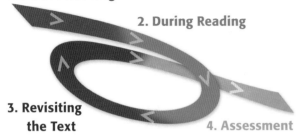

2. During Reading

3. Revisiting the Text

4. Assessment

This Teaching Version will assist you in directing children through the process of reading.

1. **Begin with Before Reading** to familiarize children with the book's content. Select the skills and strategies that meet the needs of your children.

2. **Next, go to During Reading** to help children become familiar with the text, and then to read individually on their own.

3. **Then, go back to Revisiting the Text** and select those specific activities that meet children's needs.

4. **Finally, finish with Assessment** to confirm children are ready to move forward to the next text.

Before Reading

Building Background

- Write the word *brave* on the board. Read it aloud. Ask children for examples of people who have done brave things. Ask children if they have ever needed to be brave, and invite them to share their experiences.

- Introduce the book by reading the title, talking about the cover illustration, and sharing the overview.

Building Future Vocabulary
Use Interactive Modeling Card: Sentence Maker

- Introduce the word *move* by writing it on the Sentence Maker.

- Explain that box 1 is for a *character,* box 2 for an *action,* and box 3 for a *place.* Ask children if *move* is a *character, action,* or *place.* (action)

- Use the Sentence Maker to create a sentence.

Introduction to Reading Vocabulary

- On blank cards write: *slide, garden,* and *brave.* Read them aloud. Tell children these words will appear in the text of *Brave Little Snail.*

- Use each word in a sentence for understanding.

Introduction to Comprehension Strategy

- Explain that as you read a story, you can guess what might happen next (predict), and you can check your guess (confirm) by reading further.

- Tell children they will be stopping at different points in *Brave Little Snail* to make predictions about what will happen next. Explain that they will also be checking their predictions as they read.

- Using the cover illustration, ask children to predict why Little Snail might need to be brave. List the predictions on chart paper.

Introduction to Phonics

- Write the word **up** on the board. Read the word aloud and use it in a sentence. Point out that the word begins with the letter *u* and the initial sound /u/, which is called a short *u* sound.

- Give several examples of words with initial /u/. List them on the board, point to the letter *u,* and read each word aloud.

- Write a sentence on the board that includes several initial *u* words. Have children identify and read the words that begin with the letter *u.*

Modeling Fluency

- Read page 3 aloud, modeling adjusting pace by drawing out the word *slide.*

- Point out that the italicized type is used to set the word apart from the other words. Tell children they can show this by reading the italicized word in a different way.

2 During Reading

Book Talk
Beginning on page T4, use the During Reading notes on the left-hand side to engage children in a book talk. On page 16, follow with Individual Reading.

During Reading

Book Talk

- Explain to children that the cover and the title page provide clues and information about what is going to happen in the story.

- **Comprehension Strategy** Ask *Do you think the story will be a happy story or a sad story?* (happy) *How do you know?* (The snail is smiling.)

Turn to page 2 – Book Talk

Brave Little Snail

By Anne Giulieri

Illustrated by
Kiera Poelsma

Future Vocabulary
- Say *Compare the cover and the title page. They are almost exactly the same. What is different?* (The background on the title page is white; the cover has scenery behind Little Snail.)

Now revisit pages 2–3

During Reading

Book Talk

- Ask children to share what they know about gardens. Have them describe any gardens that they have seen.

- **Comprehension Strategy** Ask children to predict what things Little Snail might encounter in the garden.

- Have children locate the words *garden* and *slide*.

- **Fluency Skill** Point out again that *slide* is in italics. Ask *How did that affect the way I read it?* (You read it slowly.) Explain that the way you read *slide* also mimicked how Little Snail was moving. Say *I read the word like I was sliding.* Have children practice reading the sentence.

Turn to page 4 – Book Talk

Here is Little Snail.
Little Snail is in the garden.

2

2

Little Snail likes to *slide.*

3

Future Vocabulary

- Point out the shell on Little Snail's back. Talk with children about how snails carry their homes on their back. Ask *What other animals carry their homes on their back?* (turtles, tortoises)

- Say *Compare Little Snail in these two illustrations. Why has the illustrator drawn him differently on page 3?* (to show that the snail is moving)

Now revisit pages 4–5

3

During Reading

Book Talk

- **Comprehension Strategy** Tell children that they can now check their predictions about what Little Snail would encounter in the garden. Ask *Did we predict that Little Snail would encounter a big leaf? Does it make sense to predict that Little Snail could encounter a big leaf?* (yes) *Why?* (because there are usually leaves in gardens)

- Ask *How do you think Little Snail feels here?* (He is scared.) *How do you know?* (from his expression in the illustration) Ask children to predict what Little Snail will do about the big leaf and why.

Turn to page 6 – Book Talk

Little Snail is looking at a leaf. The leaf is big.

4

Little Snail is not big.

5

Future Vocabulary

- Say *Here the author is comparing the size of Little Snail to the size of the big leaf. What other things could you compare on these pages?* (the snail and the flower; the leaf and the flower; different colors)

- Say *Sometimes we use compare in a different way. For example, when something is really, really good, we might say that it is "beyond compare." Is there anything that you think is beyond compare?*

Now revisit pages 6–7

During Reading

Book Talk

- **Comprehension Strategy** Say *Little Snail decided to go up the big leaf. Did that surprise you? Why?* Review their predictions of what Little Snail would do about the leaf.

- **Phonics Skill** Have children locate the initial /u/ word on this page. *(up)*

- Have children locate the word *brave* on these pages. Ask *Why do you think Little Snail is being brave?*

Turn to page 8 – Book Talk

Look at Little Snail.
Little Snail is going
up the big leaf.

Up goes Little Snail!

6

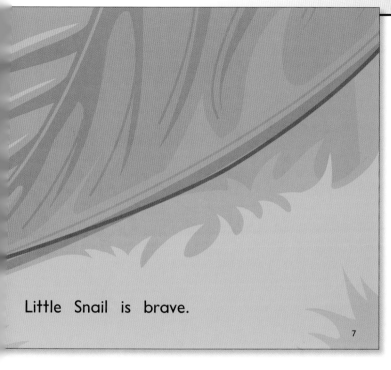

Little Snail is brave.

7

Future Vocabulary

- Say *Little Snail is moving again; here he's going up the leaf. Does a snail move slowly or quickly?* (slowly) Discuss with children how a snail moves.

- Ask *What do you imagine it would be like to move around with a shell on your back?*

Now revisit pages 8–9

7

During Reading

Book Talk

- **Fluency Skill** Ask *Which words did I read more slowly?* (*up, up, up*) *Why do you think I read them that way?* (because the snail is going up slowly) Point out that the *up* text rises to mimic the snail climbing.

- Point out the boldfaced type for the word *is* on page 9. Explain that this is used to emphasize the word.

- **Comprehension Strategy** Say *Little Snail is on his way up the leaf. Raise your hand if you predict that he will make it all the way to the top.*

Turn to page 10 – Book Talk

Little Snail is going
up the big leaf.

Up, up, up he goes.

Little Snail **is** brave!

9

Future Vocabulary

- Point to the snail's shell and remind children that the shell is also the snail's home. Say *Snails get to take their home with them, but sometimes people have to* move *from one home to another. Have you ever had to* move *to a new home? What was your favorite part of* moving?

Now revisit pages 10–11

During Reading

Book Talk

- **Comprehension Strategy** Say *Little Snail made it all the way to the top! Why do you think he was able to climb the leaf?* (because he was brave)

- Say *Now raise your hand if you predict that Little Snail will stay at the top of the leaf. What do you think might happen to him now that he is there?* (He might fall.) *What makes you think that might happen?* (Little Snail looks worried or scared.)

- **Phonics Skill** Have children locate the word that starts with the letter *u*. (*up*) Ask them if it is a short or long vowel sound. (short)

Turn to page 12 — Book Talk

Little   Snail   looks   up.

10

10

Little Snail looks down.

11

Future Vocabulary

- Say *Compare Little Snail's expressions on these pages. How do his feelings change?* (He goes from happy to worried or scared.) *Why is he scared?* (because it is a long way down)

- Point to the edge of the leaf behind Little Snail. Say *If he moves back, he will fall off the leaf.* Explain that this is another meaning for *back*. *Sometimes we have to move back a seat or chair. Can you think of times when you have had to move something back?*

- Point to the snail's trail. Say *This shows us the snail's trail as he moved up the leaf. Why can we see Little Snail's trail?* Explain that snails leave behind a streak of slime wherever they go.

Now revisit pages 12–13

During Reading

Book Talk

- **Comprehension Strategy** Say *So, we see that Little Snail did not stay at the top, and now he's rolling down the leaf. Do you think he will be okay?* (yes) *Why?* (He is inside his shell; the grass is soft.)

- **Fluency Skill** Ask *What was different about how I read the words* down, down, down? (You read it faster.) *Why do you think I read it that way?* (because the snail is rolling down fast) Point out that the *down* text falls to mimic the snail going down the leaf.

Turn to page 14 – Book Talk

Oh, no!
Little Snail is going down.

Down, down, down he goes.

Oh, Little Snail!

13

Future Vocabulary

- Ask *In which direction is the snail moving?* (to the left or to the bottom of the leaf) *How can you tell?* (from the lines behind the snail)

Now revisit pages 14–15

During Reading

Book Talk

- Have children locate the word *garden* on these pages.

- **Comprehension Strategy** Have children point to Little Snail in the illustration. Say *We can see that Little Snail is in the* garden. *Can we tell yet if he is okay?* (no) *Why not?* (We can see only his shell.) *How can we find out if he is okay?* (by reading the end of the story)

- Refer to the list you created earlier in the lesson. Review with children their initial predictions about why Little Snail would need to be brave.

Turn to page 16 – Book Talk

Where is Little Snail?

14

14

Is Little Snail in the garden?

15

Future Vocabulary

- Have children look at the pictures of Little Snail on pages 14 and 16. Say *Compare these two pictures. Do both of these pictures show Little Snail?* (yes) *How do we know this is Little Snail in the first picture?* (We can see a little bit of his shell.) *How do you think he feels in the first picture?* (scared, nervous) *How do you think he feels in the second picture?* (relieved, happy)

Go to page T5 — Revisiting the Text

15

During Reading

Book Talk

- Leave this page for children to discover on their own when they read the book individually.

Individual Reading

Have each child read the entire book at his or her own pace while remaining in the group.

Go to page T5 –
Revisiting the Text

Look! Here is Little Snail!
Little Snail is safe.

16

During independent work time, children can read the online book at:
www.rigbyflyingcolors.com

Revisiting the Text

Future Vocabulary

- Use the notes on the right-hand pages to develop oral vocabulary that goes beyond the text. These vocabulary words first appear in future texts. These words are: *back*, *move*, and *compare*.

Turn back to page 1

Reading Vocabulary Review
Activity Sheet: Word Sorter

- Tell children to write the word *garden* at the top of the Word Sorter. Ask *What do you think of when you hear* garden? List the responses.

- Have children choose two categories for the words and write them in the second row. Then have them sort the words into the categories.

Comprehension Strategy Review
Use Interactive Modeling Card: Story Map

- Write *Brave Little Snail* in the center box of the Story Map. With children, determine the story elements and record them in the boxes.

- Review the story elements and have children discuss which ones they were able to predict and why.

Phonics Review

- Using page 8, have children locate the initial /u/ word and read it aloud. *(up)*

- Ask children to list other initial /u/ words. Have them write a sentence using one of the words.

Fluency Review

- Ask children to read the text on page 8. Remind them that the snail is going up slowly.

- Ask volunteers to read the text on page 12. Remind them that the snail is rolling down fast.

Reading-Writing Connection
Activity Sheet: Venn Diagram

To assist children with linking reading and writing:

- Have children use the Venn Diagram to list items found in a vegetable garden, a flower garden, and both gardens.

- Tell children to find a phrase in the story about something found in a garden. Have them copy it into the appropriate part of the diagram.

T5

4 Assessment

Assessing Future Vocabulary

Work with each child individually. Ask questions that elicit each child's understanding of the Future Vocabulary words. Note each child's responses:

- If someone asks you to take a step back, should you move closer or farther away?

- Would you say a painting is a moving picture? Would you say a video is a moving picture?

- Compare day and night.

Assessing Comprehension Strategy

Work with each child individually. Note each child's understanding of making and confirming predictions:

- When you read the story's title, what did you think Little Snail would do in the story? Why?

- When Little Snail first saw the leaf, did you think he was probably going to climb it or turn around? Why?

- Was there something in the story that made you think Little Snail might have a problem when he reached the top?

- When were you sure that Little Snail was okay?

Assessing Phonics

Work with each child individually. Spell *up* using letter tiles. Have each child read the word aloud and identify the initial sound. Tell each child to use letter tiles to create and read aloud three other initial /u/ words. Note each child's responses for understanding initial /u/:

- Did each child read initial /u/ correctly?

- Did each child easily identify initial vowels?

- Did each child successfully create new initial /u/ words and read them correctly?

Assessing Fluency

Have each child read pages 2–3 to you. Note each child's understanding of adjusting pace:

- Was each child able to slow down and draw out the word *slide*?

- Was each child able to read other text at a regular pace?

Interactive Modeling Cards

Sentence Maker

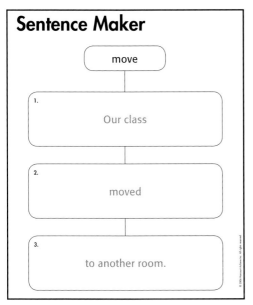

Directions: With children, fill in the Sentence Maker using the word *move*.

Story Map

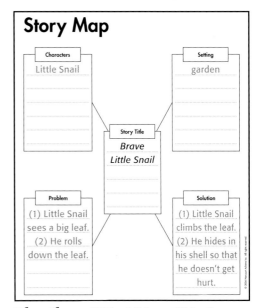

Directions: With children, fill in the Story Map for *Brave Little Snail.*

Discussion Questions

- What did Little Snail encounter in the garden? (Literal)
- How did Little Snail protect himself when he rolled down the leaf? (Critical Thinking)
- How do you think Little Snail felt when he reached the top of the leaf? (Inferential)

Activity Sheets

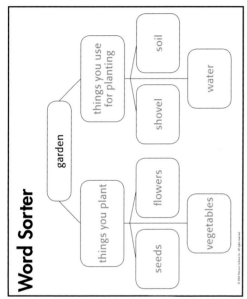

Word Sorter

garden

things you use for planting
- soil
- shovel
- water

things you plant
- seeds
- flowers
- vegetables

Directions: Have children fill in the Word Sorter for *garden*. Have them chose a way to categorize words describing *garden*s and write the two category titles in the second row. Then have children sort words into the appropriate category.

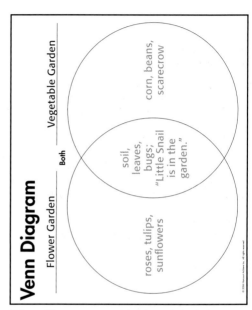

Venn Diagram

Flower Garden | Both | Vegetable Garden

Flower Garden: roses, tulips, sunflowers

Both: soil, leaves, bugs; "Little Snail is in the garden."

Vegetable Garden: corn, beans, scarecrow

Directions: Have children label the Venn Diagram *Flower Garden* and *Vegetable Garden.* Then have them write things they would expect to find in each garden. Have them list shared things in *Both.*

Optional: Have children copy a phrase from the story into the appropriate part of the diagram.